Table of C

Preface

My book is for anyone who wants to learn how to grow a super-healthy amazing vegetable plant known as rhubarb and supplement your diet with a healthy alternative to store-bought. This vegetable is also frequently used and eaten as a fruit, especially in pies and jams. You'll learn everything you'll need to know on growing this amazing plant, jam-packed in this short but thorough book! Join me on a quick, easy to follow step-by-step guide that will bring you rewards for a lifetime!

Chapter 1

Consider Growing Rhubarb

Health Benefits

Rhubarb is an amazing plant composed of nutrient-rich vitamins and minerals that our bodies lack so much these days! This plant contains a lot of vitamin C, which helps immune support. Also, it contains a total of fourteen vitamins and ten minerals! This super-food truly has it all. When consumed, you'll find the secret to feeling healthier and much younger! (Nutritional Data) In many health-science publishing's, the more natural unprocessed foods we consume, the reversal of age becomes much more apparent. I know I want to be on the side of feeling better and younger, so please join me in enriching your knowledge on such a great plant!

Growing and supplementing your food/diet nutritiously,rhubarb is such an easy plant to grow, and with the right knowledge, it's crazy not to propagate and use it at your home. When cooked correctly, this plant can be one of the most enjoyable vegetables or appetizers to consume. One plant can grow into many plants if you start with a good foundation of soil, nutrients, water, and care. On average, one can grow this plant in pots, soil and raised beds, making it exceptionally versatile. One small, raised bed in your backyard can produce pounds and pounds of delicious vegetables that you and your family can preserve or freeze to enjoy all year long!

When you add this food to your diet regularly, you'll notice yourself starting to reap the benefits such as better digestion; this is partly due to containing a large amount of fiber. You'll notice you get over colds or being sick much faster, thus improving your whole bodily functions. Buying this food in the store, if you can even find it will cost you, on average in stores, you'll pay a decent amount for something naturally grown which won't have near the quality as if you grow your own due to a lot of chemical fertilizers and sprays being applied to a store-bought product. One could save a grocery bill or more by growing this yourself over the course of a year if you eat it regularly. Start-up growing costs are negligible for this delicious reward!

Spend Time with Family, Start a Tradition

Have you always wanted to get outside more? Or maybe you've wanted to give your kids something that you never did growing up. Regardless, isn't it nice to think back to our childhoods and remember fond memories of having a garden in the summer, and having fresh fruits and veggies at a moment's notice? Tell me you can't get any fresher than going out your door and harvesting something in your backyard. I can recall having a garden every summer. My family was big on that. It supplied us with something to do as kids, and my father and mother enjoyed having one. Not to mention having saved us hundreds, maybe thousands of dollars over the years in grocery bills and supplied us with much healthier foods overall. I want you and your family to have a chance to make fond memories like I did and learn a valuable fading skill in our society today when most people have a tough time growing a plant on their window sill! Let's get back to our roots and mother nature and get to growing!

Spend More Time Outdoors

Do you remember playing outside on those long summer nights when you were younger? Remember all the fresh air and sunlight you got, maybe even a few sunburns, well with a little sunscreen you were good; nevertheless, our bodies need Vitamin D. This key nutrient is one of the most lacking nutrients in the American society alone! Vitamin D is responsible for strengthening our bones, allowing better calcium absorption from our foods, and even aiding our immune systems.

Gardening and growing your food will not only provide you the obvious benefit of "free" food, but it will also allow you to reap the benefits of the great outdoors even if you live in the city, thus allowing your body a crucial vitamin that is severely lacking today. Help yourself out and your family and start a new traditional legacy! Let's get growing!

Chapter 2

Different Varieties

What is Rhubarb?

Rhubarb, scientific name (Rheum rhubarbarum), is a plant that grows best in colder climates, recommended for USDA hardiness growing zones 3-8. This plant features celery-like stalks with gigantic leaves growing out of the ends of shoots. These plants grow bulb-like in the soil sprouting prolifically once rooted well and given ample water, nutrients, and compost. **Caution: The leaves** of this plant are highly toxic, and you must never consume them!!! The leaves contain high amounts of oxalic acid, as well as high amounts of calcium and potassium oxalide salts. The edible part you can eat is the stalks. These plants prefer a moist, highly rich soil high in compost or decomposed manure type of environment.

Different Varieties

Cherry Red scientific name (R. x hybridum) This variety had bright red stalks, which are one of the sweetest and least tart of the rhubarb family. Since this variety is sweeter by nature, you'll probably need less honey or sweeteners, FYI. This variety does well in USDA zones 2-8 and does very well in the Northwestern U.S., particularly Northern California, Oregon, and Washington. Grows to 3 feet tall and wide at maturity.

Chipman's Canada Red- is another type of red variety. It is very sweet by nature as far as rhubarb is concerned and grows robustly to 3 to 4 feet tall by wide and does best in USDA hardiness zones 3-8. This variety was developed in Canada and does its best in Northern latitude gardens.

Crimson Red- My preferred variety. This variety I grew up with all my childhood, loving the semi-sweet tart flavor this variety provides. This variety is known as The Northwest variety and does best in cool, damp climates, like Oregon. The stalks on this plant stay their crimson reddish color all growing season, making it especially appealing to the eye and landscaping features. Grows 3 to 4 feet tall by wide. This variety makes wines very well, too, as my mother would use it in her recipes to make some of the best berry wines I've tasted. You can grow this variety in USDA hardiness zones 3-8.

German Wine, scientific name (R. x coltorum), is known for making some great berry wines. This variety grows a little smaller, keeping to 2 to 3 feet tall by wide, making it more ideal for container growing. It features pinkish reddish green stalks, giving it a unique look in the landscape. This variety grows in USDA hardiness zones 3-8 and is a sweeter variety.

Glaskin's Perpetual is a variety that can grow in slightly warmer areas, hints USDA hardiness zones 3-9, and prefers cooler areas. This type ripens a little earlier than its brothers and sisters giving you a slightly earlier harvest starting in the spring going into summer. This variety is ideal for container growing as it only gets about 2 feet tall by wide. It keeps its sweeter flavor throughout the growing season better because it has less oxalic acid in the stalks vs. its counterparts. This characteristic leaves you with a sweeter plant for longer, versus its counterparts start to get more bitter through the summer due to oxalide acid increasing.

Hardy Tarty is an heirloom variety (meaning it's been around for many years). This type can tolerate warmer climates despite having a USDA hardiness zone of 3 to 8. Hardy Tarty is by nature very tart, so it can be consumed throughout the whole growing season as it doesn't get any more tart as the season goes on versus springtime shoots.

Holstein's Bloodred–This variety is the reddest of the rhubarb family, often working well in pies and desserts due to its color and taste. It boosts large juicy blood-red stalks, making it a pleasant look in pies. This variety is also a producing champion, often netting 5 to 10 pounds of rich stalks per plant each year! This plant will grow 4 feet tall by 5 feet wide if happy. It grows best in USDA hardiness zone 3-8 and likes lots of sunshine. Pie lovers indulge; this is your plant!

Kangarhu–This variety was developed in Australia, hints its unique name specifically to endure heat and warmer temperatures better than the others. This one grows best in USDA hardiness zones 4-8, though it handles some heat better than the rest. This variety produces a stalk that keeps its unique red color even when cooked and is also a tart one. Kangarhu will grow 3 feet tall by 3 feet wide.

Prince Albert - This variety has been around for over a hundred years! Respectfully named after Queen Victoria's husband, this heirloom does best in USDA hardiness zone 3-8, growing 3 to 4 feet tall by wide. This variety is best harvested in the spring from early April to later May for the best flavor. Prince Albert makes an exceptional pie-filling or jam, highly recommended for those purposes.

Riverside Giant (aka the cold man)–This variety is the cold hardiest of plants enduring temperatures down to -40 degrees Fahrenheit. Growing in USDA hardiness zones 3 to 8 or down to 2 if in cold frames over the winter months. This variety is a mini giant growing up to five feet tall by 4 feet wide. If you got time to wait, it's not a bad choice for colder areas or a growing seasonal hedge. Beware: It takes about three years before you can start to harvest this plant due to its slow starting growth.

Sunrise–This variety does exceptionally well for freezing, canning, and preserving for the year. This characteristic is due to having thicker pinkish stalks, which negate freezer damage from happening as much, and is less prone to becoming mushy in the freezer. Grows in USDA hardiness zones 3 to 8 and gets 3 feet tall by wide.

Timperley Early (for hotter climates)–This variety does well for those in zones 8 and above that still would like to grow rhubarb. Early can be grown indoors reasonably well, making for an excellent chance to get an early harvest even in February if done correctly. It grows to 2 feet tall by 2 to 3 feet wide. This variety is known to some as one of their favorite varieties to eat and cook!

Victoria is one of the most popular worldwide due to being the first rhubarb varieties consumed by people. The plant was first founded at the start of Queen Victoria's reign over Great Britain in 1837. It's a popular heirloom variety due to its versatility. This variety does well in a galore of uses from pies, dressings, jams, or desserts. The plant does well in many conditions and boosts nice green-reddish stems.

How It Tastes, Best Recipe

Rhubarb is a vegetable technically, though it's often considered a fruit, and it tastes like one if sweetened correctly. Rhubarb makes a great addition to any side dish if honey or sweetener is used for cooking it. You can also make a great pie by mixing rhubarb and strawberries together, one of the best I've ever had!

When eaten, this plant is crunchy if not cooked and tastes very tart and or sour. If mixed and steamed with honey and water, it tastes like a sweet, unique tasting fruit. The only real way to describe the taste is to tell you to try some. A tasty recipe to follow is 1 cup chopped rhubarb (chop into 1 to 2-inch pieces). Add 1 cup of water if open stove steaming it, if using lid just over half a cup should suffice. Then add three tablespoons of raw honey. The tastes can vary slightly due to the time of harvesting the plant and the amount of honey added. If that's too sweet or not sweet enough, I recommend adjusting your honey amounts up or down. If your end product is too watery, you can steam a little longer, or just take note and add less water next time.

Your end product should come out with a slightly semi-soft texture, about the same texture as stiff applesauce.

Like I said, if it's also not jam-like enough for your tastes, add a little more water. It's a straightforward recipe to follow, also taking little to no time to cook. Once steaming, it should take no more than 10 to 15 minutes to steam into a jam-like substance. If you want an excellent rhubarb pie recipe, Betty Crocker has some good ones to follow. There are countless articles about this online as well. Once you taste this plant, you'll never go back. It's a real summer treat!

Ease of Growing

Rhubarb commonly grows best in partial to full sun (6-8 hours a day) of light. It does best in deep rich silty clay loam soils high in organic material. I've had the best success growing it by planting in a raised bed, partially off the ground, and mulching with a lot of horse manure covering the bulb heads. This plant loves nitrogen (it's the N on the N-P-K labels on fertilizers) due to its fast growth rate once established. Once planted, just keep watered amply, keeping the soil moist, and keep well mulched every year with rich compost, and you'll have the best-growing rhubarb! This plant grows best in cooler climates where it grows as a perennial (aka it comes back every year), or it can be grown as a winter annual in Southern areas of the United States as well (meaning it dies every year living once). Rhubarb likes lots of water, though it also likes well-draining soils as it doesn't like being flooded. It can be grown in containers as well and in raised beds. Once planted, if done correctly, this plant will take off in a couple of growing seasons.

Know Your Climate

Rhubarb is a plant that requires almost a cooler climate to grow at its best. This is partly due to its huge soft leaves that transpire and lose a lot of water to evaporation in the sun. As stated earlier, this plant does best in USDA hardiness growing zones 3-8. If you're unsure of your growing zone, just look it up on https://planthardiness.ars.usda.gov/PHZMWeb/. This site will tell you which zone you are in based on your general location in the states. These hardiness zones get updated over the years as certain zones change over time. I have found that if you can grow legumes and squash well in your area, you could probably grow rhubarb well as it likes similar conditions. Not to fear, though, if you're out of this zone, you'll just need to care extra for it if in a really hot or dry area, allowing a lot more shade and heavy mulch and water. Your plants may only live one growing season in these conditions, mainly in the winter due to dying in the hot summer months.

Chapter 3

Best Time to Plant

Know Your Area

I can't understate this; some places warm-up before others, like the South versus the North. Depending on what area and latitude you're in, this difference can sometimes be weeks or even months. Planting when everything is still dormant will yield the best results! (Dormancy is when all the trees and plants are in a slowed growth stage, most lose their leaves and "dieback," not actually dying, just slowing way down on growth).

Best Time

Depending on your area, you'll want to plant just before the spring if possible; early spring also works too. The reason you must target this time of year is due to the plant just about getting ready to grow, which will situate it in its permanent home before it starts growing for the season, ensuring it's not shocked as bad. This time of year will also allow your plants to save energy in their roots to be strong by the time winter sets in, helping aid in growing again next year.

Rhubarb grows roots mainly laterally, so it's key to plant with compost if the soil is lacking and place compost over the plant heavily, which will really get your plant growing and keep it protected during the winter months. Think of planting your plant in the spring as somebody giving you a year to train for a marathon versus only one week; what's realistic? Treat your plant similarly, and you'll be heavily rewarded.

Less Watering and Maintenance

Keep with this schedule, and you'll save countless hours in the garden just trying to keep your wilted plant alive if planting in the summer months. Help yourself out by keeping with planting in dormancy or just coming out of it to relieve yourself of taking hours more babying your plants with extra watering on top of what you'll already be doing.

Earlier Harvest

When started earlier, harvest your plants earlier due to plants becoming established much faster under favorable conditions for establishing a good root structure. Who doesn't love to enjoy their harvests weeks and even months early? It sounds like an easy choice!

Chapter 4

Soil Conditions Required

Rhubarb's Preference

By nature, this plant loves rich, well-draining soils consisting of lots of silty loam and partial clay types of soils. Not to worry if this isn't your type of soil, as you can enhance your existing soil by making some easy adjustments.

How to Check Your Soil

You can dig into your soil and note if your soil seems very dense, sticking together well, and not draining quickly, chances are you've got lots of clay in your dirt. This type of soil is prevalent in lowland bottom areas or near slow-moving waterways. Suppose you've got this soil plant in a slightly raised bed by working composted steer or horse manure into your soil, about a two-part compost with one part native soil on your site. This will help feed your plants and get their roots out of the standing water in the wet months to make sure their roots don't rot!

If your soil is a moderately soft structure holding together in chunks then breaking apart easily, you've got a silty loam or silty clay loam soil, chances are. This soil structure is preferred, as you must make the least amount of adjustments to hit that favorite spot. Add a 1 to 1 part soil to composted manure in the soil. You have the option to create a raised bed or not, as drainage isn't a problem.

I've found a raised bed is still good in almost all cases as it creates a nutrient-rich smaller area where you can easily keep weeds and other plants from growing with your plants. Next, if your soil is of a sandy structure not holding together, you must amend your soil with lots of good water holding manures and compost such as steer or horse manure with rotted hay or alfalfa. You can also use a sawdust mix with manure to save money. The goal here is to hold water in your soil for as long as possible so it doesn't leak out and your plants wilt and die off from a lack of water.

In this soil, you'll need to add preferably a 2 to 3 parts compost manure mixed to 1 part of your native soil to achieve proper water retention. Don't cheap out on these amendments as your plants will surely not do as well, and you're only hurting yourself with less harvest, or perhaps losing your plants to extra stress.

Make Your Future Easier

Plant your rhubarb in a good location in proximity to your house so you can avoid having to carry water or loads of compost. Place your plants in an area that already has the above better conditions as much as possible to enable yourself to put in less effort modifying soil structure and still get a great harvest. If you've got a mostly afternoon sunny spot in a slightly raised area with better drainage and richer soil structure naturally, use this to your advantage, thus saving you more time and money.

Chapter 5

Lighting Requirements

What Light Allows

Sunlight allows for your plants to go through a process in which they self-process and create their own food called chlorophyll. This is created through exchanging nutrients, water, and CO2 (Carbon). This then creates the chlorophyll for the plant, and then the chlorophyll is what the plant uses to absorb sunlight effectively to grow and produce lots of energy in the form of fruit. When you take sunlight out of this equation, you are disregarding a very critical step, and your plants will undoubtedly suffer or die off.

Increase Yield

Increasing your yield for harvest is huge! One must assess their situation by looking at the plants' needs and seeing the light, nutrients, water, and mulch available to your plants. Once you get these items in a balance, you'll reap excellent results, one which will repay multiple times over. Take a quick survey of your garden or yard and see where the sun rises, where it stands midday, and where it sets. Remember, the sun always rises in the East and sets in the West. From March through June, the sun is highest in the Northern hemisphere, and the opposite is true for the Southern hemisphere, having its highest times from September through December. For those of us residing in the U.S. or Canada, the first will apply to us and for anyone about parallel to our latitude.

Best Place to Situate

Rhubarb loves full sunlight (defined as 8 hours of light per day). Some situation dictates when only partial is better (defined by 6 to 8 hours of light per day).

Northern Hemisphere

Up North, your weather is much milder in temperature and light compared to the southern and middle states. You'll want to give your plants one of the sunniest spots in your garden. You'll want to ensure to situate your plants in a sunny location in colder northern climates where they'll receive maximum afternoon sunlight through the day.

Southern Hemisphere

Down South, you'll be constrained with the weather as well, just the opposite end of the scale. You're going to need to shelter your plants from the hottest afternoon sunlight, generally from 3:00 pm, and onward in the afternoon, you'll want them getting only partial sun. By allowing the morning and early afternoon sunlight, your plants will still get plenty of light, though they will be well sheltered from the brutal heat of the sun, preventing them from getting scorched later in the day.

Chapter 6

Water Requirements

Rhubarb's Preference

Rhubarb prefers moist, well-draining, rich soils filled with lots of compost. You'll know your soil is moist when you can stick your finger in the soil or peel back the top few inches of soil and see darkened wet to the touched soil if you have this type of soil perfect! If you don't, do not stress; here's how to fix it!

What's Your Soil Like

Dry to Touch Sandy: If this sounds like your soil, you must incorporate rich moisture retaining composted mulch and manure into your soil and raised beds. Do this, as stated in Chapter 4. This will create a new environment that will hold water particles much longer and better.

Dry to Touch Dense Clay: If this one sounds like your soil, it will be a hard-super dense material when dry, super mushy, and a soggy sponge-like material when wet. This type of soil is not preferable, as it will create an environment where your rhubarb's roots will get root rot. (Root rot happens when a lack of oxygen gets to your plant's roots due to the soil not allowing air particles easily into the soil, thus killing your plants from water suffocation). To rectify and fix this, create a raised bed, mix in equal parts composted manures, and mulch with soil to allow sufficient ground room from existing soil grade to get those roots out of that toxic environment!

Somewhere in the middle: If this sounds most like you, that's a good sign. You'll have to do the least amount of work. Your plants will probably already grow in the soil as is, though to do exceptionally well, you'll want to incorporate well-composted manure still and top-dress with ample mulch to provide good nutrients while still holding adequate moisture in the soil.

Watering

You'll need to apply a ready supply of water to your plant via traditional irrigation or drip irrigation. Expect that your plants will need about 2 to 3 inches of water per week during the growing season through the summer and a little less during the spring. When it's super warm, you may need more than this. This is just an average. If you don't get considerable rain, then you'll want to supply water, or your plants will succumb to wilt or even death.

Things to Remember

Soil is a science and skill of art. You'll surely need to figure out what works best in your location, though these practices from above will certainly get you close to the best success. The best way to improve your soil is by doing it yearly, maintaining and adding more compost and manure to the soil, and keeping developing good soil culture. In doing this, you'll constantly be building up your soil structure and increasing microbial activity (Mycorrhizal is a fungus that's been around since all plant life) and improves nutrient exchange by increasing the roots of plants. If you put more back into your soil than you take out (which is heavily disregarded today in common practice), you'll always be getting a better harvest every year!

Chapter 7

Mulching and Compost Requirements

Keep it Rich

Rhubarb loves a nutrient-rich environment heavy with lots of nitrogen, promoting its lush leafy growth and stalks. Give it that!

Cheap way: The best way to get manure and mulch at the same time, usually on the cheap, is to go to your local horse stable or local farm and ask if they've got any manure or used animal bedding material you could take off their hands. Most places would be happy to get rid of this as it's a chore to do constantly, trust me. I know we had horses and cattle. Make an agreement with them, whether they already have it piled up or you have to scoop it up. Regardless of this, most if not all times, you'll be able to get a whole pickup or trailer load for next to nothing! Doing this could save you a lot of money! Most of these composts will not be fully composted, though if it's horse manure, it's alright; you can apply it right away. If derived from cattle manure, then you'll need to compost for a few months if not already composted before applying, so time this accordingly.

Pay-for Way: This way can often be the easiest and involves just purchasing already bagged composted manure at your local garden store. In doing it this way, you'll avoid problems such as weeds in the compost most of the time, and you'll have an easy-to-use product in a reasonably mess-free bag. Caution: If doing a large area, consider doing the first way, as you'll likely save hundreds of dollars. On the other hand, if you're just making a small area or raised bed, this way usually is the most convenient.

Layer

Layering is a process where you apply different mulches or composts at different levels when applying to soil. The best method is to do your planting mix out of a mixture of native and good topsoil if your soil is very bad, manure, and composted mulch. After that, you should top-dress plants with a little bit of composted manure, then apply a well-composted mulch consisting of one of the following: rotted hay, straw, sawdust, bark mulch, or the equivalent. Once this is completed, you'll have successfully layered your plant's soil. Layering helps provide better decomposition within your topsoil, encouraging natural worms and microbes to break down and live within all the different layers of soil. Also, it protects from having an odor from the manure if covered by mulch. Another thing is if your mulch isn't fully composted, it will suck nitrogen out of your soil, this is a natural process when decomposing, by having on top of the manure and out in the air, it will reduce contact with your plants, and not allow nitrogen to be depleted from them as there will be a barrier between roots. The uncomposted mulch will draw more nitrogen and carbon out of the air instead of your soil.

Constant Improvements

Continually improving your soil gives the added benefits of easier growing, fewer plant deficiencies, and less overall symptomatic problems. Ways to stay on top of improving soil quality are to do an annual compost and mulch buff to the planting area. Add and replenish any amounts of compost that decomposed over the course of the previous year in the fall and or winter just before spring growth. If you continuously improve your soil by adding to it annually, you'll be surprised just how well your plants will start doing in a few short years. Also, you'll be moving into long-term sustainment your kids, and their kids can be able to enjoy, now that's something!

Feed Your Soil, Feed Yourself

I cannot reiterate this enough if you feed the ground that your plants draw nutrients and minerals from, you'll, in turn, be providing better, higher quality, denser, nutrient-rich foods for you and your family. Another thing that's good about feeding the soil is it will always come back to you tenfold. Not only will you produce better crops, but you'll also use less water, use less fertilizer, and take less time to provide a fantastic product!

Chapter 8

Fertilizer Requirements

How to Read A Fertilizer

All fertilizers have three numbers on the front of them. These numbers are as follows N-P-K. These stand for nitrogen-phosphorous-Potash. Nitrogen promotes lush leafy growth for the plant. In terms of rhubarb, they are heavy nitrogen users, and it helps with strong stem structure and leafy growth. The plant's root system uses phosphorous, and it helps promote large healthy roots for your plants. The plant uses potash for overall plant vitality and absorption of plant minerals and nutrients and aids in development.

Helpful Tip: The most common lacking nutrient in most garden and agriculture soils is nitrogen. Nitrogen is one of the most used nutrients for plant growth; it quickly diffuses into water by most means; therefore, it runs off soil smoothly. A simple soil test will show soil deficiencies and excesses. Therefore, I highly recommend them for new gardeners to get an idea of the general area you're working with and what you'll need to focus on improving in your landscape. A simple way to get one done is ordering a kit online or contacting your local county cooperative extension service and paying a small fee to have them analyze a soil sample of your ground to get an idea of how your soil is composed. These can sometimes be the best means of cost savings as you'll find out if you need to be spending extra on fertilizers and or composts to achieve good plant growth.

I place a strong emphasis on soil culture as nutrients that are out of balance in your soil will surely be noticed by your plants! Be careful when you select a fertilizer to select based on your plant's needs in that type of soil, deciding if you would like to stick to a more natural or chemically derived approach to feeding your plants. The following will list some benefits and drawbacks to both.

Benefits of Nitrogen (Nitrogen-P-K)

- This is the most common issue that rhubarbs lack, getting enough for healthy growth.
- Essential for production as it's a key protein enabler in biomass production.
- Allows for lush leafy-green growth in the whole plant.
- Quicker growth, avoiding stunted growth.

Plant Indicators of Nitrogen Deficiencies

- Plant leaves very light green and small and then turn yellow during the growing season.
- Purpling leaves can show a nitrogen issue, also a chance of a phosphorous problem.
- Shortening and smaller leaf petioles as compared to normal, turn a reddish color. Don't mistake the color change during the fall months when leaves die back and sometimes turn a crimson color based on weather.
- Plant's midterm and older growth leaves will show signs first as new leaves will use all available nitrogen, cannibalizing it from older growth. If a nitrogen deficiency is suspected, you can take tissue samples from older growth to have sampled at your local cooperative extension or equivalent to test them.

Organic Sources of Products Naturally High in Nitrogen

- Blood Meal (Approx. 12% nitrogen by content, fast-acting to absorb).
- Fish Meal liquid (Approx. 10% nitrogen by content, fast-acting

to absorb).

- Feather Meal (Approx. 15% nitrogen by content, also slower to release).
- Alfalfa Meal (Approx. 3-5% nitrogen by content, a more balanced fertilizer, slower to release overtime).
- Bat Guano (Approx.10% nitrogen by content, fast-acting).

- Chicken Manure (Approx. 3-6% nitrogen by content, fast-acting, caution as it can burn if not composted).

Benefits of phosphorous (N- phosphorous-K)

- It supports vigorous root growth.
- It supports in small ways for stem production.

Plant Indicators of Phosphorous Deficiencies

- Purple leaves and veins on leaves can indicate a phosphorous deficiency
- CAUTION- Use only in small amounts as excess can cause water contamination via water runoff into lakes, increasing algal blooms resulting in less oxygenated water and a toxic environment for fish.

Organic Sources of Products Naturally High in Phosphorous

- Bone Meal (Approx. 15-27% phosphorous by content, slow to release error on the side of less than too much will throw off plants' growth easily).

- Bat Guano (Approx. 3% phosphorous by content, quicker to release).
- Crab Meal (Approx. 3-6% average phosphorous by content, slower to release, gardeners, love due to containing a natural chemical called chitin, a natural bug repellant).
- Alfalfa Meal (Approx. 0.5-1% phosphorous by content is a more balanced fertilizer with a slower release).
- Rock phosphate (Approx. 20-33% phosphorous by content, not as uniform for quality as unique rock formations have different nutrient contents, reasonably slow to act as it's long-term).

Benefits of Potash (N-P-Potash)

- Plants grow healthier, aiding in water and nutrient uptake.

- Plants using less water.
- Less disease and insect-prone.
- Produce more bountiful crops.

Plant Indicators of Potash Deficiencies

- Brown and yellow spots and or discoloration around the edges of the leaves.
- Leaf curling includes iron Chlorosis (usually due to the soil's pH being too high above 6.8).
- Plants seem stunted, even with nitrogen-rich soil additives. This is evidenced by a lack of potash in the soil.

Organic Sources of Products Naturally High in Potash Sources

- Kelp (Seaweed) (Approx. 4-13% potash by content, quicker to release) contains approximately 60 trace minerals as well to boost, though be careful to follow application rates as a little of this goes a long way.
- Hardwood Wood Ash (Approx. 3-7% potash by content is quicker to release small amounts at first). Be careful as this will also increase soil PH.
- Greensand (Approx. 3% potash by content. It has a slower release since it is not as water-soluble). Be careful as this will also increase soil PH (natural element derived from a mining element process containing up to 30 minerals to boost).

Chemically Derived

They make this type of fertilizer from chemical substances, and is not a natural means of feeding your plants. Plants will still register the food as the same as the natural counterpart, though. Chemical types of fertilizers will feed your plant; however, it won't feed your soil, though the plant won't recognize the difference between chemical or naturally derived nutrients. A good article by *EnviroIngenuity* reiterates this well, "Plants cannot distinguish between an organic or synthetic fertilizer–the nutrients are processed in the same way. However, the similarity stops there. (*EnviroIngenuity*) That being said, your plant will not notice, though your soil will notice. The beneficial organisms living in it, helping aid your plants in growth, will severely take note and could suffer.

Tip to keep in mind with this approach is that when you feed your plant, you're not just feeding your plant, you are feeding your soil, and your soils really feeding you. Ask yourself this question in a lawn setting. This isn't as crucial in using unnatural means as you're not eating the grass, hopefully. Though you're going to be consuming this product's fruit, it begs to question using that which has no value to your soil health. Take a skin product. For example, the chemical may work better in some accounts for removing blemishes, though ask yourself if you really want to chance consuming harsh chemicals into your body. The connection can be made that you're not actually consuming these harmful nutrients though I've always realized that if the plant absorbs them and uses them in its growth, they are still a part of that fruit.

Instructions on most of these types recommend wearing masks and glove, which sounds like it may be hard on your soil too? Realize that the same is true for natural means like blood meal, or bone meal, though those recommend it mainly for your skin and avoiding animal by-product issues. Chemical fertilizer is available to the plant the fastest, which is optimal. However, on the flip side, it could also burn the plants a lot easier. It by-passes all the natural processes of decomposition via the microbial activity, which would help the plant consume the nutrients, thus lowering if not killing these beneficial workers in your soil. Always ponder the idea that states, "We are what we eat," and our plants are what they eat in part; therefore, take caution on using this fertilizer if consuming for food. This type has benefits such as quick absorption, ease of application, and good consistent results. It's up to you to decide if it's right for you.

Naturally Derived

Helping your plants and soil out in one simple go by using naturally derived fertilizer is best for good soil to plant equilibrium. When I say natural, I'm not saying you must use organic or anything like that if you don't wish, just use something that is plant or animal-derived rather than that in which is derived from chemical bases. These types of fertilizers are what nature and God intended for people to use. These types come in the form of manures, kelp, blood meal, bone meal, cottonseed meal, a mix of these, or anything derived from plant or animal products. These substances are excess when either processing animals or raising animals via manure or plant-derived like cottonseed meal or kelp. These types of nutrients will feed your soil and your plant sustainably. With natural types, you'll probably notice your plant requires fewer fertilizer applications, less water, and more heat and drought resistance.

The reason behind all the above is quite simple: when you feed your soil, these natural soil building amendments you're feeding the healthy microbial activity in your soil and helping promote them to grow and produce, which your plant relies on for a healthy growing environment. Also, naturally derived nutrients usually take more time to become available to your plants fully. This could be good or bad if you need a lot of nutrients quickly, though their useful life once applied is much longer. On the flip side, the chemical counterpart only feeds your plant and often kills these organisms or hinders their essential role due to death by chemical. It's important to note that plants won't create a healthy relationship with mycorrhizal fungi when chemical means are used. These fungi also enable your plants to grow bigger, healthier roots, which allows them to absorb nutrients tenfold. Arguments for both sides can exist; realizing this, it's up to you to decide. Lastly, it's important to note that chemically derived fertilizer came about during the start of large-scale farming as it was easier to produce on a large scale for food and gave a consistent feed to plants; still worth noting though it's lack of long-term soil improvement is a tradeoff for aiding in only plant growth.

Know What's in It! Why You Should Care!

Chemical Types

Derived through "man-made" processes, which usually are derived from the excess petroleum industry, examples of the nutrients are Ammonium Nitrate, Ammonium phosphate, Superphosphate, and Potassium Sulfate. These types are then fortified with some trace minerals for the plant. Remember that plants need more than just pure nutrients to survive, including needing organic matter and living organisms that this type doesn't support. An article of studies by *Envirolngenuity* states this well "The application of a synthetic fertilizer actually kills a significant percentage of beneficial microorganisms. These tiny creatures are responsible for breaking down organic matter into a stable amendment for improving soil quality and fertility. Some convert nitrogen from the air into a plant useable form." (*Envirolngenuity*) This is important because these important workers break down all the mulch and compost you apply to your soil, and without them, nothing would get broken down to useable nutrients. Why hinder that? Also, I don't know about you and your families, but I don't want my family to eat a by-product from the chemical or petroleum industry. It's great for cars though I'm not sure about for indirectly ingesting.

We're already consuming enough of our limited supplies, such as plastics and manufacturing. Why use it anymore? Also, these derived types often lower your soil's pH. Another thing to look at is the excess that runs off into water systems, which is another reason most water is becoming more acidic, harming other parts of our water systems. (pH is the scale from 0 to 14 judging how sweet 14, or how sour 0 your soil or water is). Look at this article by Hunker The over-use of chemical fertilizers can lead to soil acidification because of a decrease in organic matter in the soil. Nitrogen applied to fields in large amounts over time damages topsoil, resulting in reduced crop yields. (Hunker). Chemicals have their times and uses, such as when you're not ingesting it like a yard of grass; also, it's more cost-efficient for big-scale farming. From all the previous stated, if you want this for long-term sustainable food production, it shouldn't have that big of a place, especially in your home garden! Grower beware!

Natural Types

They are derived through naturally occurring substances coming from animals, plants, and element formations. These types of nutrients don't rapidly feed your plant. Instead, it releases nutrients a little at the start and then overtime feeding your plant, which is more ideal by reducing excess water pollution runoff, also lowering your fertilizer costs. Microorganisms usually are found in healthy compost-rich soils, in which they convert organic nitrogen into inorganic nitrogen, a process called mineralization. The plants then can absorb this form of mineralization of inorganic nitrogen. Here, you don't cut out the middleman! :) This middle man works and does all the heavy lifting to ensure healthy nutrients and minerals are available to your plants.

Follow the Old Saying of Getting What You Pay For

When purchasing something that you'll use on a plant and then consume, please be careful, as the goal here is to increase the nutrients in your food and get a better product than the gigantic producers. The Department of

Agriculture did a study in an article by Hunker stating, “According to data produced by the US Department of Agriculture Nutrient Data Laboratory, foods grown in soils that were chemically fertilized were found to have less magnesium, potassium, and calcium content.” (Hunker) Simply put, the choice is yours; choose to increase your soil’s powerful workers in the form of beneficial microbial life with naturally derived nutrients or not. This is a rather deep decision though increasing your fruits’ nutritious value would seem most definitely worth it!

Chapter 9

How to Plant

Items You'll Need

- Shovel/and or spade
- Gloves (optional)
- Water can/ and or hose with water
- Topsoil (if your native soil is very bad)
- Compost of your choice (more on this in Chapter 4)
- The mulch of your choice (more on this in Chapter 4)
- Fertilizer
- Markers (if wanting to label) if planting more than one variety I recommend.
- Weed barrier if desired, heavy mulching will negate most weeds, though.
- Shelled nutshells (optional if you have a severe slug problem)
- A little bit of sweat and work��

Procedures

1. First, you'll want to try to plant on a partly overcast day. Try to plant later in the day, as this will allow your plants to rest overnight. By doing this, it will stress your plants less.
2. Next, bring all the above supplies needed to the site you're going to be planting. (This will make your life a lot easier).
3. Mark out your spot you want to plant, whether it be in a raised bed

or, if not, already done.

4. Remove all weeds from the area if weeds are very bad, prepare your site months ahead of time by placing matting or newspaper over the area, thus suffocating and killing most of the weeds.
5. Start digging. Reference Chapter 4 for soil mixtures and applications based on your type of soil. Though, as a rule, this is the time you'll amend and mix in any new topsoil, and about half of the manure required mixing into the soil, turning it, and working it well into the soil.
6. (Disregard if using Chemical fertilizer) Mix in about half of the recommended fertilizer if using a fertilizer besides the manures to the direct soil area where the plant will be going.
7. Dig a spot in the freshly turned soil for the plant.
8. Take the plant out of the pot and scratch the roots' sides, untangling any circling roots, thus promoting them to go out and down into the soil.
9. Backfill soil around roots, keep a consistent pattern filling on all sides, slightly compacting to eliminate air pockets, ensuring soils all around roots without damaging roots.
10. Apply the rest of the composted manure if doing a top dressing discussed in Chapter 4.
11. (Disregard if using Chemical fertilizer) Apply the other half of the fertilizer if you used the natural fertilizer. Spread evenly and don't allow to touch the plant's base, keep about half a foot of distance from the plant not to harm the plant, or encourage inner rooting (if all nutrients are by the stem, it won't grow bigger roots outward as much).
12. If you want to use a weed barrier, now is the time to apply it. Cut out an area about twice the rhubarb plant's size to leave room for the plant to grow and leaf out, then secure barrier with either stakes or using the mulch to hold it down. Caution: If using a barrier, make sure to overlap at the joints where two pieces come together at least 6 inches, or more so no weeds grow up in between the linings.
13. Spread mulch evenly over the soil around the plant allowing for 2 to 4 inches of mulch to be spread evenly across the area, taking care not to cover the plant's stem, leaving a small opening by the

stem for light to get to the plant.

14. If you have a severe slug problem, place a nice amount of shelled out cracked tree nut shells around the planting area's outside perimeter, as this will keep most slugs out. (fun fact, the shells work due to having a sharp surface which the slugs won't cross due to scraping and killing them on their slimy bellies).
15. Finally, mark plants with markings or stakes if desired, and then water in well until soil is fairly saturated. After that, you'll want to follow Chapter 6's guidelines for watering needs thereafter.

Chapter 10

Harvesting, Pruning and Storing

Before Harvest

If you notice upright stems growing, which look like flowering seed pods growing, cut them off at the base. These stems are merely the plant producing male and female flowers to produce more plants via seed. This will take extra energy away from the plant in fruit production, and seeds are usually not the easiest or preferred method to start more rhubarb plants. If you want more plants, wait two to three years and divide your plants into more plants by splitting them at the base, carefully digging around one side of the plant, do this in the late winter or early spring just before new growth.

When to Harvest

Harvesting depends heavily on when you planted, weather conditions, and overall care of the plants will dictate when your plants can be harvested. As a general rule of thumb, the first year, you'll want to leave most of the stems for the plant to store up ample amounts of energy in the roots and become established. Times for harvest vary, though judge the ripeness of the plant by the color of the stem and size. Take note that most of the ripen stems will be toward the outside bottom of the plant as new shoots typically grow on top of older stems. Take a small sample to see if it ripened to the desired preference. Try to avoid harvest into the late summer as the bad-tasting acid will be at its highest generally this time of year. Harvest within the first half of the growing season for best results. Harvest generally no more than a quarter of plants total stem mass. In years two and three, you can harvest most of the plant, as usual, making sure to never cut the whole plant during the growing season all at once as not to shock it! (Only harvest nice ripe, plump stems ready to be cut, leave the small stems).

How to Harvest

Pull or cut stems off at the base of the bulb-like plant. Take care not to rip out roots. It's best to cut off at the ground or pull-down and towards the base of the plant to pull off the main stem carefully. Remove leaves from stems before processing and eating, compost them, and or take them elsewhere as leaving dead or dying leaves behind will encourage slugs to hang around eating on your plants.

How to Store or Preserve

Depending on the variety, and the uses you intend to get out of your plants will dictate how and what method you use to store your harvest.

Freezing

This is by far one of the most common, as you chop up into small 1-2-inch pieces and place on a cooking pan with parchment paper and freeze until stiff, then stuff into a good quality freezer bag and store for up to a year. By freezing before placing into a bag, you'll negate chunks sticking together, and a more uniform, easy to work with product. This is an excellent method if you want to store for future cooking and pie-making, or just dessert dishes.

Jam

This is another useful method, as you'll steam down your stalks just as you usually would cook to the desired recipe. Once cooked into a nice jam, you'll place in good quality mason-jars and pressure cook till you get a good seal, then they are ready to be stored long term in the freezer. There are countless websites online and books out there that will show you how you can go about canning correctly. Be careful as I can't stress this enough because a bad seal on a jar could create bacteria botulism, which is very poisonous and fatal.

Summary

Before you go, I just wanted to say thank you for purchasing my book.

You could have picked from dozens of other books on gardening or the same topic, but you took a chance and chose this one.

So, I just want to say a HUGE thanks to you for getting this book and for reading all the way to the end.

Now I wanted to ask for a small favor. **Could you please consider posting a review on the platform? Reviews are one of the easiest ways to support the work of independent authors.**

This feedback provided will help me continue my mission to write these types of books and continue to help you get the results you're looking for. So, if you enjoyed this book, please let me know! (-:

In conclusion, feel free to always refer back to this book again, as the more times you read it, the more knowledge you'll gain. I wish you and your family the best adventure and the utmost success in growing amazing Rhubarb!

Printed in Great Britain
by Amazon

58164412R00030